Dedicated to my forever guardian and my little sweet pea.
Every pulse of my heart beats for *you*.

Dear reader,

May my words reach you on some visceral level and bring you a certain comfort and peace that I have spent a *lifetime* searching for…

CONTENTS

ROSE-COLORED GLASS
9

WHEN PETALS FALTER
81

ROOT ROT
111

ROSE-COLORED GLASS

Evening walks on blue flannel skies,
skipping rocks on the surface of dirt road memories,
I fused the music of graceful autumn wind
with the afterthoughts of winter solstice
knowing I'd cross paths with wanderlust again

I didn't fall for his unkempt hair,
or the ink on his arms that told stories
he wasn't ready to tell
Not the scars on his hands that only come
from foolish boys on warm summer days
Not the way I saw the forest in his eyes
when the sun hit them perfectly
Not the firmness of the arms that held me at night,
fingers in my hair as he kissed me goodnight
No, I fell for the softness of his gaze,
crippling my soul to pieces as delicately as fallen petals
I fell for the realization that years from now,
when I have grown old and tired and
my memory somehow escapes me,
my heart will always come back to him

I only ask that you love me without regret,
that you accept that I am broken and may not last
that you look upon me with adoration
that you fight to keep me safe
I have lost my light
but I have spent my life in waiting
waiting for you
longing for you
writing poems for you
dreaming of you
I have waited for you to take me
dreamt of your lips pressed upon my cold mouth,
as I inhale a soft sigh
patiently, I have waited for you
and I shall be homesick for you
even in heaven

How I long to touch you
No darling, not in the way you think
I long to touch you with the taste of my pen
Unbutton your body and seize your heart
How I long for you to take me to bed with you
No darling, not in that way
I long for your hands upon my folded pages,
my words at the edge of your lips
How I long to satisfy your longings
No darling, not in the way of flesh
I long to ease your restless nights,
undress your mind and fill it with a bewitching ink
Leave you so enraptured,
that you crave even my empty pages,
so long as they're in my hands

Poetry = midnight scribbles of last minute thoughts and emotions
while my soul is half-sleeping
Pieces of me that I lost along the way that I forgot to jot down.
when it mattered most = right as rain

She was not one to be tamed,
her passion could never be bridled
She is riveting, she is wild,
a mind raw with magic
She is a poet

If anything, I only wish to be the tattered memory
of the girl you stole glances at
with a sheepish grin and flushed cheeks
The one you never spoke to,
but who still haunts you in your dreams

There's romance in December
Snowy kiss extract
Balsam stirred in weathered marrow
Mistletoe crooning to touch us both
Crossbones enlivened in my chest
Symptomatic of red and green plaid
Damned to the memory of frozen feet
upon winter's fate

Never accept the fate of false friends
Even if it leaves you in a dark room by candlelight,
a cigarette in your mouth and a pen in your hand
You don't need an audience to watch you fall,
but your fans will stare in awe to watch you rise

There is no shame in solitude
Sometimes, when the world becomes too loud,
or has dealt you more pain than your heart can handle,
you need to retreat to that forest of quiet within your mind
Go for a walk
Live there for a time if you must
The world will be waiting to see you again
Be kind to yourself

Fall for a woman who wants to know
the depths of your soul,
so that she may fill it with hers
Your pockets matter not

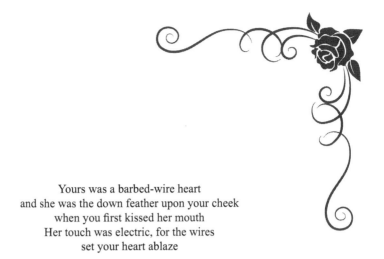

Yours was a barbed-wire heart
and she was the down feather upon your cheek
when you first kissed her mouth
Her touch was electric, for the wires
set your heart ablaze

Oh, how I love the cold of winter
But I have dreams of the spring
Spring whispers that dead things will be made new again
Plant me, o springtime
Grow me into a lovely thing
the hummingbirds will envy
A sobering beauty steeped in the scent of a rose's breath

Her embrace is crippling, my heart unzipped
Her gaze makes me blind, in my eyes the stars aligned
She is the figure in hazy dreams,
the warmth in a once empty bed
She is the earth clutching fallen leaves,
the promise of amber-colored skies
She is the silence broken from a shackled mind,
the destination of my soul's wanderings
She is the potted root of a planted seed,
reaching from my chest of dreams
So violently she took me,
and so gently calmed my storms

She was lost, broken
Finding solace within the pages of other shattered poets,
feeling their words on the tips of their pens
A self-prescribed seclusion on the rims of empty glasses,
memories flicked off their cigarettes
Then she found him within their words,
breathed a sigh of relief and said,
"There he is…"

She thought she was ugly
but she never saw the flowers that bloomed
in her eyes when she talked about poetry

She's not a woman, she's a warrior
Her armor the breath of steely blooms

The sandman has my dreams written upon his watch,
for he knows your voice is my only lullaby
as you cradle my heart to peaceful slumbers

She was a woman who kept things tidy
But her soul..was another matter entirely

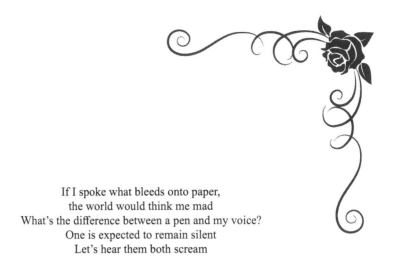

If I spoke what bleeds onto paper,
the world would think me mad
What's the difference between a pen and my voice?
One is expected to remain silent
Let's hear them both scream

How is it that you were so tangible a dream,
I still couldn't see you?
It was not until you drifted from my dream to my bed
that I strained my eyes to wake and found you
tangled in my dream catcher

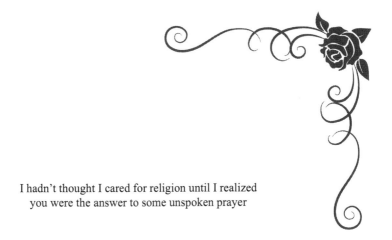

I hadn't thought I cared for religion until I realized
you were the answer to some unspoken prayer

There was a sweetness in her heart
that even hummingbirds craved

I hold tired memories of him in my pocket,
as dark little secrets my pen will whisper later

Her body was young, but her soul was old
Like a wildflower in the sand,
she had weathered many storms
Yet he still found beauty in all her dried petals

Why do they trap fireflies in glass jars?
How strange a thing to encase a fire that's
meant to spread the wishes we've made

She was an ardent lover of books
Taking different poets to bed with her each night
And each night, they had their way with her soul
It was a delicious form of promiscuity

Theirs was a forbidden romance,
one born of blurry passion
They had their secrets, disguises,
hidden in places where only darkness and beauty reside
He knew the contours of her soul when he fell into her eyes,
deep within the crevices of her flesh
And so she took him, laden with darkness,
lifting him in solitary breaths of ecstasy
She knew the magic of controlling forces of gravity,
for he fell under her spell while even staying still

And so, the sun fell in love with the moon,
though he'd never seen her face
She possessed a beauty the other planets envied
Writing her letters in the stars, the sun implored,
"Do you think we could be lovers?"
somber was her reply,
"No darling, it is an impossible romance."
Yet, he felt her close, a lingering allurement of
her presence, though she were miles away
His words sang through the galaxies,
traveling light years, in hopes of a chance
meeting with she who possessed a porcelain face
She needed no letters, for she felt him too,
the warmth of his inner fire lighting her way
He knew she'd find him across the great divide
And so, the moon fell in love with the sun
It was, an impossible romance

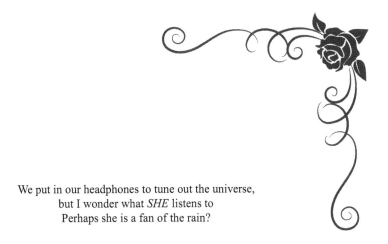

We put in our headphones to tune out the universe,
but I wonder what *SHE* listens to
Perhaps she is a fan of the rain?

I relished in the possibility that I might belong to you
Where was my mind in all those forsaken dreams?
Freed, in your arms

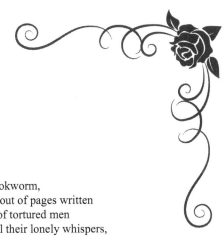

She was a bookworm,
weaving her way in and out of pages written
from the insomnia of tortured men
Burying herself asleep in all their lonely whispers,
she felt the textures of their silence in the cold of her sheets
Their requiems were her lullabies

Not even an eternity of sunrises could keep me as warm
as the touch of your hands

Oh darling,
If I were to ever undress my soul to you behind closed doors,
You'd never lay your hands on me

All it took was one taste of her heaven,
and all he wanted was to dine upon her soul
So that he may know Paradise

I loved you without warning
And it was a love so intense,
I didn't care about me so long as my light
was infused with your blood

Then one day, she recognized him
And her heart abandoned her and whispered,
"This is the place..."

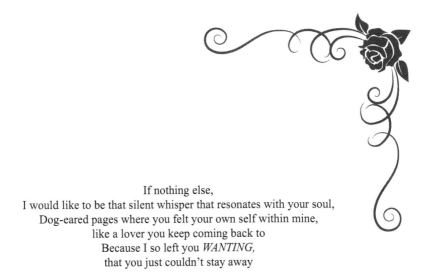

If nothing else,
I would like to be that silent whisper that resonates with your soul,
Dog-eared pages where you felt your own self within mine,
like a lover you keep coming back to
Because I so left you *WANTING,*
that you just couldn't stay away

If you find yourself in a state of unrest,
take my peace of mind
I don't need it
I lost it somewhere in all these ink-filled pages

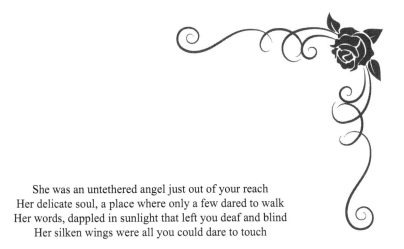

She was an untethered angel just out of your reach
Her delicate soul, a place where only a few dared to walk
Her words, dappled in sunlight that left you deaf and blind
Her silken wings were all you could dare to touch

You felt like a dream even I
could not find in my sleep
Dear god,
if his arms are where I am meant to be,
I never want to wake up

In this sacred space of a steadfast love,
Only the touch of parted lips and whispered nothings can keep us safe
Don't leave
Those out there are trying to crack the code to this beautiful thing
STAY

Just for today,
choose to honor your soul
and feed it lines of poetry like sugar in your tea
Leave the bitterness of coffee for tomorrow

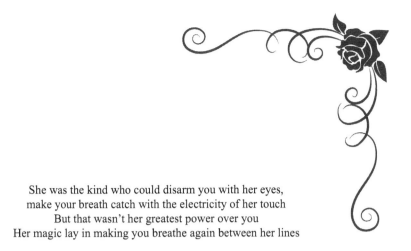

She was the kind who could disarm you with her eyes,
make your breath catch with the electricity of her touch
But that wasn't her greatest power over you
Her magic lay in making you breathe again between her lines

Love yourself so fiercely that not even a mirror
can remind you of your beauty

Would you meet me near the stars to make love beneath the moon?
May we leave the planets stupefied
as we pierce through their notions of time and space?
Your skin the taste of constellations,
as your gravity holds us afloat
Such a dream as this, to wake in presence of the stars again
and wipe their dust from your cheek

When I was a girl,
I dreamt of kissing frogs and princes to save my heart
When I was a young lady,
I wished for a bad boy with shadows in his eyes
When I was a woman,
I hungered for the end of my search for the symmetry of man and wife
When I was a wife,
I went to bed in peace

It used to drive me mad the way you'd leave your things behind
Your towel on the bathroom floor,
leaving trails of steam streaking down our mirror
Your sweater draped over your chair,
with traces of cologne that assaulted all my senses
A half drunk bottle of your favorite ale,
where I knew your mouth had been
It was enough to drive me mad
But there was something about the things you left behind
that always bring me back to you

My voice speaks in whispers,
so I asked my pen to do all the screaming

To my dear stranger:
It is my deepest hope to reach you on some euphoric plane of existence
That my words arrest your senses
That my ink-blood may transfuse
only the sweetest visions of me within your mind
And when you find yourself drifting off to that silent, tranquil slumber,
you will only taste the ghost of me upon your tired lips

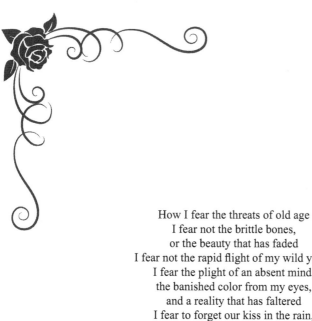

How I fear the threats of old age
I fear not the brittle bones,
or the beauty that has faded
I fear not the rapid flight of my wild youth
I fear the plight of an absent mind,
the banished color from my eyes,
and a reality that has faltered
I fear to forget our kiss in the rain,
The scent of roses on our bed,
or the sound of your name upon my lips
from those nights of ecstasy
I fear a random rock that sits upon my finger,
photographs of strangers upon my bedside table
I fear the company of a silent roommate on a chair next to mine,
fighting to bring me back
And so, should I entertain the presence of something larger in the skies,
I pray that when this body betrays me,
and my spirit is consumed by the clouds,
All I see is your face dancing across my memory

There is no need for the clothing of this weary flesh,
that which oppresses both mind and body
There is no use in imitating the sun and stars with my decorated words
They'll take away my treasured books and toss my diamonds to the skies
For when I come upon the gates of Heaven,
the only question they will ask is if I walked the earth
with an unfaltering love within the center of my soul

I learned the complexity of romance in the poetry of dead men,
and figured that your arms were the safest place to land

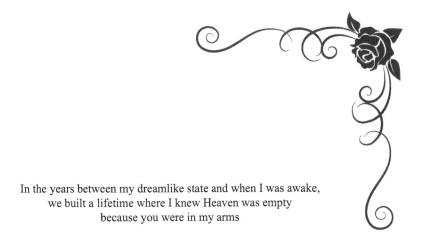

In the years between my dreamlike state and when I was awake,
we built a lifetime where I knew Heaven was empty
because you were in my arms

They fell for each other in summer,
when tensions were high upon fevered brows
They fell in sync with the ebbs and flows of sunlight on the horizon,
deep-rooted within the hazy wisps of golden clouds
Warm winds swaying both their hearts to whisper fires upon their bodies,
conscious of their carnal surrender
Summer heard in their laughter,
Summer tasted in their kiss,
Summer felt among their limbs
They never slept, for the sunset was their pre-ordained fate,
a romance bloomed with the chaos of the trees
Both summer air and unified breaths arose to meet the August moon
They fell for each other in summer
It must have been the heat

He found her beautiful,
but not in the way that most men hunger for
She was not beautiful in the luscious curvature of her form,
peaks and valleys he longed to trace his fingers over
Nor the way her jade eyes captured the very marrow of his bones
She was not beautiful in the way her crimson lips,
those tearful rose petals,
curled into a smile that invited his own mouth to latch upon hers
She was beautiful for none of those things
She possessed the kind of beauty that poets write about on silken pages,
each line a dagger to their hearts,
Though a worthwhile death for their inherent longings
He saw beauty in the hushed tones of her voice, a muffled music
that when it drifted in his ears,
it sent him into a dreamlike stupor, drunk upon her words
An intoxication that only occurs after too much wine
Yet she carried no arrogance about her,
unaware of the beauty that she seemed to inhale and exhale
into the bodies of dying men
Therein lay her beauty
She remains unaware, eyes lowered,
in the hopes that she'll go unnoticed
How I long to drink her in

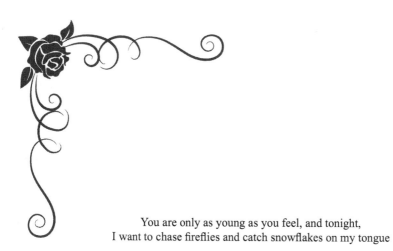

You are only as young as you feel, and tonight,
I want to chase fireflies and catch snowflakes on my tongue

He was a saint and a sinner in his own right,
but I longed for his embrace
So I held my hand outstretched
from the spacious clouds of Heaven,
in hopes that he might reach back

I loved him as the autumn and how he out-lived the beauty immortalized in fallen amber leaves

Not even the dead of sleep could fade the beauty of her
that I fought to replicate in my dreams

And when their souls merged by way of parted lips,
Heaven's angels hushed, in pausing of their song
For even they knew twins souls so cosmically in tune
were rare among the soils of earth

It provides me a great sense of comfort,
that now, when I go to take your hand,
I am reaching for home

My hope for you when you take a stroll on these tiny scraps of paper
is that you will see something beyond this existential flesh

And she was so lovely that even the gods were at war
over the realm of her dreams

Find the one who sees fire in your eyes and lights a match

I'd prefer the kind who lay their hands upon my soul
more so than the flesh on my body

My only wish for you my love,
is that you arrive upon sleepless nights so torturous
that they are filled only with thoughts of me

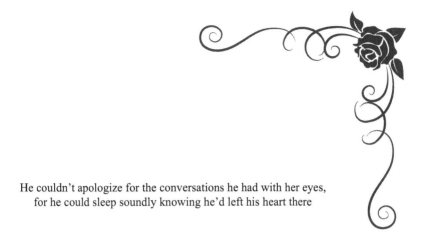

He couldn't apologize for the conversations he had with her eyes,
for he could sleep soundly knowing he'd left his heart there

She longed to represent something soft
Not in texture, but soul
To be a source of light only for him
To restore a faith long ago lost to the wicked,
gray skies of this vast landscape
She longed for his desire to touch invisible wings,
drowned within Heaven's shores at the sight of something so hopelessly
unflawed

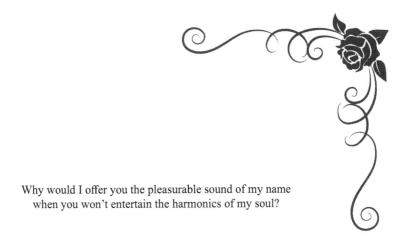

Why would I offer you the pleasurable sound of my name
when you won't entertain the harmonics of my soul?

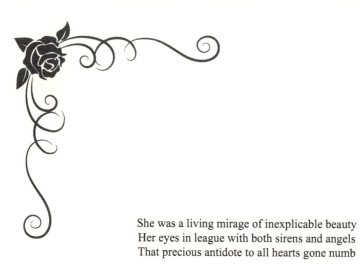

She was a living mirage of inexplicable beauty
Her eyes in league with both sirens and angels
That precious antidote to all hearts gone numb

WHEN PETALS FALTER

There was a certain sadness in her kiss,
the way she shuddered at his hand upon her alabaster cheek
But he loved her anyway
He loved her anyway

The girl from yesterday?
She was one of the good ones
The sight of whom could kill the darkness of my vibe
The sound of which could silence the commotion in my head
and cast feelings of anger aside
Dealing my soul a tender blow,
she kissed me straight out of Hell

For the love of all that is gray and uncertain:
If nothing else,
lay down your sword and let the scent of every flower you smell
usher your hand to hers, say it,
and watch as everything changes color

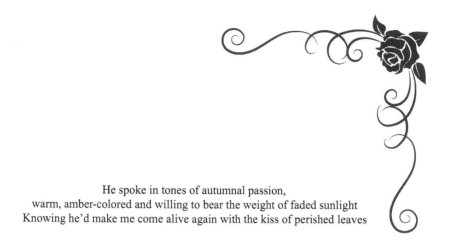

He spoke in tones of autumnal passion,
warm, amber-colored and willing to bear the weight of faded sunlight
Knowing he'd make me come alive again with the kiss of perished leaves

To kiss her was to taste the sun,
but she was a creature of the night
Never abiding by the rules of daybreak
And each morning when he kissed her again,
he wondered where she'd been,
for she carried the bite of wolves

It was one of those things that happened without warning
Like being grabbed by the sleeve from behind and kissed
in the middle of New York city traffic
Blurred, but filled with every color
that had since been absent from my cells
My hair turned dark chocolate
My eyes, emerald and jade
My mouth, blood red
My skin, soft ivory
The rest was still black but that was just you melding with me,
and it was the perfect way to die in a city that never sleeps

I so craved to kiss you just once
To know what it felt like to press my mouth to yours
To kiss you with so much passion that it sent away your pain,
vanquished your shadows back to Hell,
and replaced them with the downy feathers known only to this angel's wings
To remind you that a kiss is not merely a touch of skin to skin,
but my soul holding yours down and smoothing away any creases upon
your heart
That to kiss you was to wage your broken heart for a mended one,
write poetry with my mouth and deliver it in the space between your parted
lips
For to leave you with only the most tender kiss was to quiet your heart,
body, and soul with an ardent prayer that I could not live another day
without your mouth upon mine

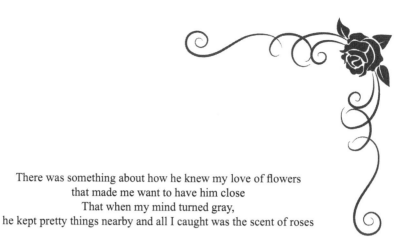

There was something about how he knew my love of flowers
that made me want to have him close
That when my mind turned gray,
he kept pretty things nearby and all I caught was the scent of roses

To be a poet is to make love to the souls
of our human counterparts
To unzip their hearts and awaken feelings of the flesh
To many, it's all nonsense, art formed with words
To us, we give you the key to our soul
as we flip through the archives of years gone by
Filling pages as the world sleeps
while we drown in tears after too much wine
A landfill of romance, heartache, loss, and regret
Seas of blood, tears, and sweat
We live by our pens, and our blood, is the ink

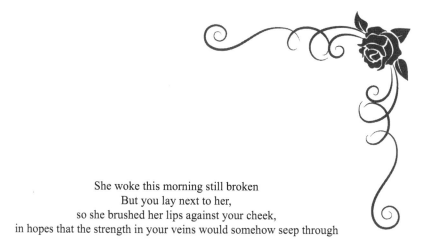

She woke this morning still broken
But you lay next to her,
so she brushed her lips against your cheek,
in hopes that the strength in your veins would somehow seep through

Out of the depths had I called unto you my love
Rescue me from sleeping death
Hold my hand as I fall from the stars,
that we may ever rest in an eternal sunrise

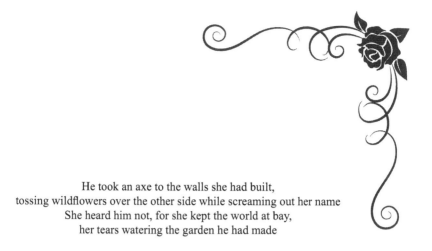

He took an axe to the walls she had built,
tossing wildflowers over the other side while screaming out her name
She heard him not, for she kept the world at bay,
her tears watering the garden he had made

I gazed upon the stars tonight thinking of you
Not because of their light, but because they (*like you*),
were surrounded by darkness, and I'd never seen anything so beautiful

Know that even if you walk away from the sun,
I will meet you at the bottom of your greatest depths
and stoke the fires that burn your soul away

I met him while half-asleep, on the soft cushions of my dreams
His face, a ghostly and melancholy charm
And as I woke, I found myself devastated at the fragments of a dream that faded,
until I looked over and saw his ghostly silhouette laying in my lap

You had Heaven and Hell in both your eyes
and I'm still not sure which I fell for

I met you under the darkest circumstances,
but all I can recall is the scent of black roses

Even if he could not hush the storms that raged within my heart,
he had the habit of placing my hand against his chest
while we both stood in the rain

Cellophane-heart protected
Withheld exhales, Sahara-dry
Combing through dark-stained summer dress thoughts
Scissors to tear-damp paper
Suspended black widow spider death
within peripheral vision
Swat
Slap
Squelch
Guardian embrace from behind, firm
Comforting
Collected cardio-swoons hidden
for safe-keeping
Pondering why he feels I am deserving of his kiss

Last night, he was kind
He let down his guard and put his sword aside
Reaching, with both hands into my soul, desperate to get closer
But it wasn't close enough, for he was miles away
Not by distance, but by heart
I knew he was a stranger to me when I looked into his eyes
His darkness was intimidating, but I danced with it anyway
It was the only way to keep me close

I hear your shattered voice call my name
Defenseless in my eyes
They cannot see you,
but my soul recognizes the chaos from within
and I wish it were mine
Your refuge found as the planets pull me closer
Find your heart settled within my words,
for I am not so far away

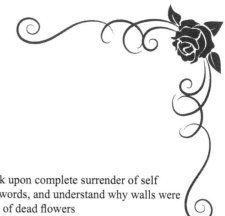

And to see his and her soul was to look upon complete surrender of self
To merge one soul with another by way of words, and understand why walls were built atop mountains of dead flowers
That a mutual melancholy had ensnared the two,
and where fate it seemed, had forced its own hand to press them both together

She had lost her voice at the sound of yet another hammer through her delicate heart
But if the breath of her song would bring her closer to you,
you would have her silence broken in waves of color within the chords of her soul

We are the rebellion to love's algorithm
We are yin and yang
We are stolen heartbeats placed in the recycling bin to be reused later when we spew garbage by mistake
We are classical music versus metal music versus Irish punk...on a good day
We are ribcages housing the haunted, but I love scary stories
We are an autumn golden tree that's been well-cared for
We are lace and burlap
We are precious metal rings in October
We are each other's cheers to "Here goes nothing." and "Here goes everything."
We are chaos and calm, though I'm not sure who's who
We are static electricity between vows
We are a puzzle on the floor with feelings of uncertainty
We are the Tim Burton version of a Ken and Barbie romance
We are equilibrium

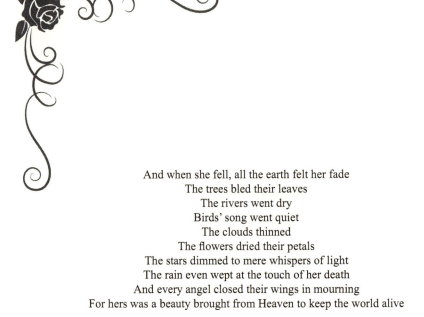

And when she fell, all the earth felt her fade
The trees bled their leaves
The rivers went dry
Birds' song went quiet
The clouds thinned
The flowers dried their petals
The stars dimmed to mere whispers of light
The rain even wept at the touch of her death
And every angel closed their wings in mourning
For hers was a beauty brought from Heaven to keep the world alive

Forlorn sobs of a downward soul,
and only he can procure the antidote to the ailments of her heart

Nightfall
I speak in tones of white and black
Compressing syllables into indecipherable speech,
a cadence only known to the rain
Sunrise
I forfeit the dead and their songs from the furnace in my ribs,
brush my teeth and spit stars from my mouth
And these eyes see in color once again

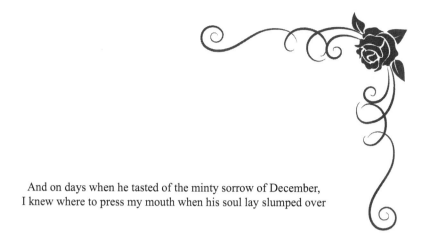

And on days when he tasted of the minty sorrow of December,
I knew where to press my mouth when his soul lay slumped over

She wrote best in the rain,
when her heart bled open
Writing only, to reach YOU
Where were you when the sky stopped crying?

ROOT ROT

I used to be summer
rearranged letters on frayed postcards sent to your chest cavity
when the sun skimmed the surface of sunflowers
I used to be spring
morning dew mouth-bound and imprinted on your memories
of the language in forget-me-nots
I used to be autumn
Nature insisting my colors change with the fading of heat,
that my veins no longer grow but wane to amber musings,
the ghost of a Mona Lisa smile trapped
between cool and frozen shades of burnt rainbows
Now, I'm just winter
Azure-boned
A chilly gothic mind half-awake from snowflake-patterned bullets,
A flightless blue bird paired with the blank stares of cold wings
trying to thaw from December's lust
I used to be,
something more, than temporary

I am 140 pounds of word-void black
falling face first into asphalt tombs,
culling through cadaver blooms plucked from a schoolgirl's heart
140 pounds of synthetic fibers of angels' traits
Shorn from rusted shoulder blades
Cut
Slice
Dice away at monotone tick tock ticks of an analogue watch
paused at the time of post-dirt skin
Mold
Silent
Gray
Dissonant spirals of burning moths aflame and the beauty in the deranged
Malignant conscience emitting white flags of surrender
on the rims of empty bottles,
Toasting to "she" who is elsewhere but HERE
140 pounds of sequential cinders flaked in order of wild colors faded:
R-O-Y-G-B-I-V, leaving noir to fend for herself
Haggard
Maniacal
Maimed
Wasted
Basted in *morte*
And 140 pounds knows how to tease them with artificial light

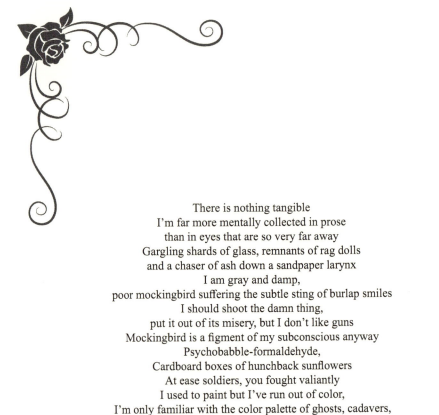

There is nothing tangible
I'm far more mentally collected in prose
than in eyes that are so very far away
Gargling shards of glass, remnants of rag dolls
and a chaser of ash down a sandpaper larynx
I am gray and damp,
poor mockingbird suffering the subtle sting of burlap smiles
I should shoot the damn thing,
put it out of its misery, but I don't like guns
Mockingbird is a figment of my subconscious anyway
Psychobabble-formaldehyde,
Cardboard boxes of hunchback sunflowers
At ease soldiers, you fought valiantly
I used to paint but I've run out of color,
I'm only familiar with the color palette of ghosts, cadavers,
the duet between flat lines and the absent pulsing of pomegranate-blood
I'm still damp, though I'm not sure if that's sweat,
blood or the stains of ink from writing too emotionally
There is nothing tangible
These non-cell brain thoughts are just passing through

Something is off-kilter
Marbles swapped out for grief-soaked saliva
Well-wish platters of filtered moonlight and ham radio murmurs
of graveyard boxes
Boo
Lying flat on an array of suggestive brain noise
Skitter
Scatter
Pitter
Patter
And my emotion-puppets line the sidewalks of self-portrait she,
But the sun didn't kiss her today
In the hollow of my rib cage,
the sun set too early again and I am the high
of cocaine minus the confusion
Nothing

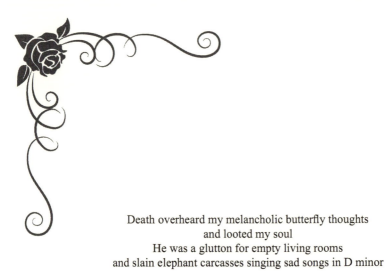

Death overheard my melancholic butterfly thoughts
and looted my soul
He was a glutton for empty living rooms
and slain elephant carcasses singing sad songs in D minor

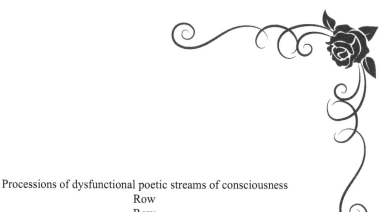

Processions of dysfunctional poetic streams of consciousness
Row
Row
Row your boat gently down the stream
The mundane juxtaposed with machine gun blues
Yesterday's garbage, the perfume of recycled black
And I'm using brain tissues to blow my nose because I'm allergic to sunlight,
perverting the art of pain over pleasure
And the idea of lace's texture teases my skin, taunts my fingers
I wish I were still soft, like raw poultry or bloody steak
Cue the exit music of UNPLUGGING and the useless taste of hospital food

Brain sick
Hack
Cough
Scratchy throat thoughts spread like strawberry red marmalade
on convex walls stitched together with poison ivy floss
10 car pileup anxiety, the eeeeeeeasy CRUNCH of pricy metal collisions
On the verge of panic button pressed,
and my demons travel in six-packs of dark ale
Off the rail cattails setting sail to my speed bump spine
Hell's nonchalant saunter into REM sleep,
Planting seeds of giddy jumps in my bed,
startling the sandman's drowsy mantra
Blink once
Blink twice
And my memory foam pillow has remembered
yesterday's insomnia and exhales it back into my skull
I wonder if people who meditate have peaceful blood flow?
Should I sleep with both legs pretzel-bent?
Super glue thumbs and index fingers together?
Ohmmmmmmmm
I forgot my tea again and I always put one sweetener packet
too little in my mug and I wonder if that's why I wake with
"Good morning" tasting so much like salt

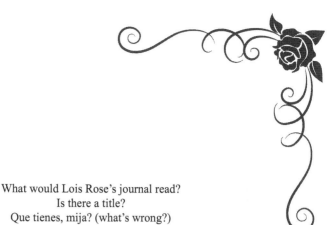

What would Lois Rose's journal read?
Is there a title?
Que tienes, mija? (what's wrong?)
Animal instinct mumbo jumbo,
incongruent subconscious party favors,
raw brain pâté smeared on crackers for hungry readers
And where's the block of rosin?
Amber colored, although mine ranges in shades of black,
the kind they use to lubricate bows prior to
caressing violin strings in empty concert halls
Cover your ears, you'll only hear sounds of
acid, semi-transparent silhouette-soul singing ballads of a dark-skinned carazón
(heart)
Llora todo que tienes que llorar (cry it all out)
No te preocupes mujer,
ni siquiera saben tu nombre real
(don't worry woman, they don't even know your real name)
They'll never know I don't do Heaven's roster justice
with these rotting wings of mine

It is so fragile a thing, the heart
Falling, ever so quickly into love
And plunging, low, low,
low into meaningless tomorrows
It conjures emotion,
a stir in my veins that leaves no room for blood

Feral angels can't survive sun poisoning
Paper wings not strong enough to fly through dead clouds
Closets full of lacy garments that look much like designer straight jackets
But of course, angels can't bleed except by lace
Despite the flood of Heaven from veins made of steel that turn to ash
And beneath the field of shoebox memories,
angels fight the gravity of night
It's not like them to cry in public

The clouds watched as she fell,
not thick enough to catch her
She was too beautiful, loved too hard
Cared too much
Gave too much
Dark she was, too, and broken
And damaged
Their softness could not save her,
and they held their breath
To weep would extinguish her flame,
but she had already went out
Her light
Her flame
All of her
Was GONE

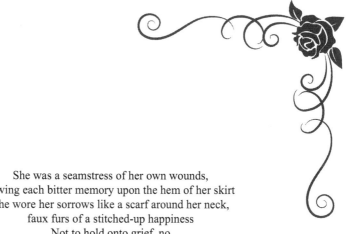

She was a seamstress of her own wounds,
sewing each bitter memory upon the hem of her skirt
She wore her sorrows like a scarf around her neck,
faux furs of a stitched-up happiness
Not to hold onto grief, no
But to remember, that even when it was expected
to rip open her seams, her heart was all that held her
pieces together

It was her moment of reckoning,
the daughter of the moon
Under a plaintive midnight sky,
incoherent was the unsung melody
of her weighted sorrows
Time is the devil who does not wait,
she she lay her ghosts to rest to regain her fire
DOWN, down with the sun

Think not of tears as a testament of thine weakness
Fear not the moments when you shed showers of tears
Close your eyes
They are but drops of rain that which fall
onto the garden of thine heart
Tears are but one of the ways in which your soul whispers
"I am still here,
I have not left thee."
Rain
It follows the winter
Melts the ice upon the flowerbed of thine heart
Soon, there will be roses

There was a blood moon a few nights ago
Just now am I thinking she was mourning
along with me

The death of her was beautiful, lovely even
No, not death, but an arresting silence
It was as if she had exploded,
a thousand glimmers in the sky
Like a faded star in the galaxy
A lonesome moon,
shaking his head in dismay at her lingering beauty
Not even death could remove her constellation in the skies
What he would give to touch her

By day, I am invincible
There is no wave that can befall me,
no blades to pierce my flesh,
no trial too tiresome to break me apart like fractured bones
By night, I am a different creature
Raw wounds gaping open
A refusal to escape the dark sheen over my mind,
the sheets of rain that drown my eyes
I've learned the language of darkness,
and by night, I let it take me
There will be light again by morning

I crave the feeling of hot water upon my skin,
coursing its way down my body
Will you melt away the dirt? Wash away this scar here,
make it so it was never there?
Scents of wild strawberry and mint,
a cool mist upon my stained flesh
Clean away all my imperfections,
the filth I hide under thick sweaters and long hair
Burn me, melt any signs that I survived something ugly
Lathered memories are washed away,
settled at my feet and turned to steam
Inhale
Exhale
And they're inside me again
Scrub
Scrub
Scrub it out
It still bleeds through my skin, the pain
Burn
Burn away

There was a time when I frequented bars on Friday nights,
the scent of whiskey on ice and putrid cigars intruding my space
I welcomed it
The noise in my mind was deafening
I needed something like a storm,
a cacophonous mix of dissonant voices
Bodies crashing, music blaring, voices clashing
But my head was louder, so I put it to paper
The ink was so intrusive, it even woke the dead

She is a poet
Yet she is also poetry, staggering aimlessly into a bar
Mixing shots of syllables, long-forgotten emotions,
re-writing romance, whiting out strangers' names,
plucking petals from flowers she's never smelled
Tasting mouths of those she's never kissed
Deleting memories etched from yester-not
Fabricated conversations with unnoticed soulmates,
making even death seem beautiful while picking fights with rhyme
And she remembers on her cigarette break
that she belongs to the night and this stupid pen
And thank God for how forgiving burning paper can be

I sometimes go to that place with a pretty house and bad dreams,
my mind a looming smoke stack
I sail into the darkness and in comes the flood
of ghosts who haunt my bones
Like a wolf of the black, I scream at the sun
Heavy lies the weight of my kaleidoscope of pain

Here I sit, in a rusty tea parlor for rosy birdies gone mad
Chirp
Cheep
Squawk
Quack
Peck, peck, pecking at the demon satellites just overhead
Flocks of sanity's hiccups, to which there is no cure
Munch munch munch on delicate lady fingers (mine),
Scratching at my beehive brain tissues,
Sneezing I'm sorrys for slapping around the face of lucid sleepy-time drink
Desperate for birdbath solitude, quiet..
Pardon the mess of expired flora and fauna of this neglected mental garden,
I should have cleaned house more
Thank God for the broad term of "calm and collected"
I hope they won't notice how closely related I am to cuckoo clocks
First impressions are everything

As he lay in a restless slumber,
He felt the scent of darkness calling in a haunting silence
He welcomed the song of dead roses in his bed
and their sonnets of the wretched,
His blissful dreams cast away from perfection,
And at 11:11, he wished that even his demons would take a knee and pray

Textured strands of black, my comfort-cloak to conceal a heart
sans the warmth of humans' touch
Dear souls, don't wake the actress whose soul is set to familiar facial lies,
Too fatigued to fein tears gone dry
Your female hopeful, always in spirit
Better late than never, they say
Rainbow patches affixed to the concept of wounds scarred over
But rainbows don't last long
And sometimes after dark, this heart loves less
Send the rivers of November rain
My heart is ready

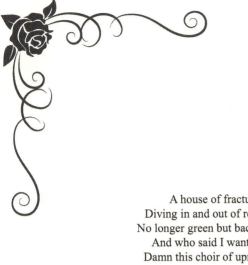

A house of fractured things,
Diving in and out of red-rimmed eyes,
No longer green but back to winter's blue
And who said I wanted those back?
Damn this choir of uprooted blossoms,
Hush your requiems, I'm not dead yet
They beg to differ, for my breaths are synonymous
with their despairing hymns
Cure her
CURE her from this damned morbid plague
I'm not dead yet

And there she sits,
upon a desert of an unwavering sadness
Dry air by day,
that no amount of tears could acquiesce by night
The ink is the same, but written on an altered hand
Her woes have claimed her weathered
Her voice speaks, though not in girlish tones,
but tones which reflect the sands of a languishing doom,
a crowded silence in her room
They name her melancholia

If I could but fill a tub with my sorrows
and be cleansed of all impurity
Bathing in my tears and drowning in its waters
Soaking in my rage, I wash my hair with all despair
Cleanse what's still left of me, oh darkened waters
Turn to lavender or mint
Here I lie, in this hazy bath of death,
I find myself renewed
And as the sun breaks through my window,
a scent of roses and milk courses through my veins
I emerge wholly unblemished,
a body untainted by strangers' hands

I am elsewhere in the trees,
perched upon the furnishings
of fragment branches, burned
It is beautiful
A gracefull mess, antique-stamped
Staggered and hungry
Hungry for perceptions of Heaven,
if there exists such a thing, lofty
Glass house transparent,
cracked-sequin cold
Look for the debris
You'll never miss me

And here I stand, at the steps of a fountain of my own tears,
cursing rusted pennies wondering,
"Why did none of you come true?"

Hoisting self up from above
winter Stockholm syndrome
Breathe in amber May honey,
cough up dehydrated leaves
Skin pales with the patience of November
to slowly take hold
Last year's family photos are in mourning
'neath layers of a bed's dust
Ebbs of pebbles down larynx roads,
flows in the certainty of throbbing sobs gasping to leave
the crematorium of my chest
Peace feigned in the depth of sleep

I hope you tell them my heart was facing skywards
Not the truth
That I died a little too much
No, put more blush on her cheeks,
she lost too much blood and all her color
Tell them I reconciled my demons and put them
in the janitor's closet next to the broken lightbulbs
that burnt out from behind my lids
Tell them I was never one who tried too hard to look alive,
that the woes of my body were all internal
Don't forget to tell them I used to sing,
not that my vocal cords deteriorated to an orchard of dead swans
I'm no longer taking requests
Tell them my mind was carefree,
that I was born in spring time May,
but that I was romantically wild as September sun
Don't mention if you looked close enough,
behind the view of my eyes,
you could see Hell's syndrome leaking from my pores and that I was always
cold
tell them that L and R were placeholders for my wings
when DOA came looking for me while I was picking flowers
Come Hell or high water, tell them I was repeated breaths of light,
Feed their hallucination,
not that I was a woman lost between Paradise and nowhere
Don't serve me transparent

Though the house be made of glass
her will is bulletproof
The windows, they did shatter following the blast
And there, you will find her,
standing tall among the debris

She had a quiet way in her beauty,
unaware of the eyes that followed her graceful gait
Her eyes never leave the ground,
for she had fallen prey to man once before
She knows that gaze,
a restless thirst for pure skin only hungry men crave
She'd been drained of her blood,
placed in a cage of gold with wings clipped short
Thank God she was an angel,
she needed no wings to fly away

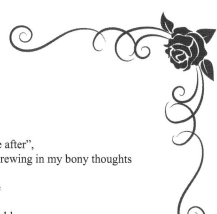

Following "the after",
there was a slightly soft hurricane brewing in my bony thoughts
Brittle
Volatile
Porous
Impressionable
And your hands
Your hands never let go of my skin
You'd think 26 years of running,
bleeding out cerebral contents, Prozac,
booze and cigarettes all sharing my dirty burdens would have quieted,
shushed the calamity
You would think…
There may be some signs of life in my pupils,
my hair, my skin, my heart
No, those are just buried remains, and the heart
Bless her, she performs the laughter of free-flowing blood
Girls like me offer sweet, stony hellos,
well-rehearsed smiles and friendly handshakes with concealed trembling mouths,
our proverbial dams holding back tear-tides and broken voice boxes
I'm sure it feels good for you to still have a faint hold
of broken-record sobs that peek from behind my vocal chords
on days when people get too close,
their gazes linger a little too long,
or my forever presses on me too firmly on rainy days
But I've learned I'm a good speller
My favorite: "fine."
F...I...N...E...
Always spat out in BOLD red ink-blood
And I really hope after "the end",
God will overlook that my body was broken FOR me not BY me,
and remind me there's no such thing as dirty in Heaven

I listen to the propaganda of dead fairies,
their rotted wings bothering my soul from conscious sleep,
bony hands swatting away at former pixies
Blood turns black, barking in my veins,
prodding my eyes toward nature's flood,
like red wine spilled on a white rug
The devil tosses trash even in my dreams,
terrifying the air with threads of gray
and when I weep,
my deluge sings flowers back to meaningful sleep

Fixed, are their eyes upon the decayed quality of my clandestine thoughts,
the lexicon of morbidity
And while the temperature of my soul's seasons are transient,
they remain, poised,
on the syllables dismissed from my quill
Be they fair-weather passengers
or loyal subjects to a humble poet's lunacy,
may they drown in the streams of this melancholic tongue

There was something I was supposed to do, but I can't remember
My head is a crowded concert hall,
a mosh pit of sweaty thoughts, cold thoughts, greasy thoughts,
crashing and burning and this girl can't rhyme
Panic attack summoned at the base of my brain stem: Showtime
Ambitions, theories, plans, ideas, thoughts,
reflections, ponderings, brooding, musings, theories...
I said "theories" twice
Make that three...all bent like paper clips and bobby pins
licked up by an angry Hoover vacuum
A fancy orchestra of buzzing bees plucking bullet holes through my cerebellum,
humming "cuckoo for cocoa puffs" like a broken record
Psyche is playing red light green light, but all I feel is red
That's cheating
Craving the bittersweet swirls of Marlboro doctrine,
and my spinal cord goes crooked,
my mosh pit quieted to burnt up candle wicks
There was something I was supposed to do,
but I can't remember
Something about elephants, empty rooms,
and this full box of matches
This is what anxiety does to my mind
She has to start somewhere

Bleached flowerbeds
Broken little hearts
A soul in famine
Crying under street lights
Slave to empty bottles
Lungs gushing with wisps of cigarette smoke
Eyes bent in winter weeping
Muted heart dappled in black
Hazes of brief romance
The sweetness of pain adrift in stormy tides
Pills that silence the mind
Empty plates
Full toilets
Blood in her tea
She's only human after all
After all?

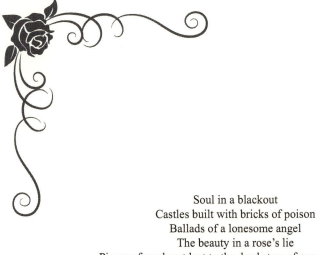

Soul in a blackout
Castles built with bricks of poison
Ballads of a lonesome angel
The beauty in a rose's lie
Pieces of my heart lost to the dead stars of empty romance
Steely-eyed devils disguised as men
Glaciers in her ribcage
Painted still-life of hope hanging on her lips
Tragic comedies in times of doubt
The intervention of her soul: the blueprints of black cocaine drawn up for an empty Eden
Spare her the fate of cloud nine

Tea gone cold
Restless sleep
Funeral dresses
Heart of a ghost
Empty lockets
Frozen pulses
Mellow mouths
Promises kissed goodbye
Swords laid down
Romantic fool's gold turned to rust
Wine: prescribed medication for sadness (*take as needed*)
Clouds over my head while praying for rain
A heart that bruises easily
The way of the sunflower: it takes a lot to make her die

Love and cigarettes
That's my poison
The cure:
Tea, ink, and a cigarette in the morning with love letters in wine bottles
tossed to sea
Balance

With a flower in each hand,
she beat upon the drums of rust-colored heartbeats
Scented not with the sobriety of the morning sun,
but a drunkard's breath of hardened midnight hours
And lilies symbolize death but her namesake
planted wings in the cells of her shoulder blades,
Don't speak of such things
She wonders if angels bleed

I want you to BREATHE me in
For once,
Don't pay attention to the thread of words on your screen
They are mere mannequins,
personified mummies displaying my underthings
Are you present with me now?
I am a puzzle with pieces missing, there's no solving me
I muse at my pores, flecked with black that are forced down my blouse
I want you close enough to feel the electricity that is ME: a gamer of words
Tremors of romance that are kneaded in my lips on occasion,
but mostly the taste of a soul forever grieved
This curve of hip that compromised my honor,
so I compose filth in prose,
pulsating corpses of dead language compressed not in ink but in HERE
That you could touch black from the branches of my veins if ONLY you
were here
Would you sit for tea?
I like mine black
And no matter what Starbucks is selling,
It's always a well of onyx atop my saucer,
with creamer and zero calorie sweetener, because a girl can hope
I am pregnant with emotions
I know how to caress your cheek with romance,
leave it black and blue with rage,
increase the heat of your blood with the scent of sensuality bridging my
flesh to yours and burn it with anguish,
Negating self with black intact
I want you IN MY EYES,
that you may worship this poetic sanctuary and know in my presence there
is also absence,
and who likes empty houses?
Make yourself at home

Where have I been today?
Roaming inner panic vocalized on paper
Making preparations for cyclic fragility of mind and body
Quite calm in retrospect of those nights when an angel was romanced by the devil,
lulled to the chill of December
And her face is reminiscent of swans,
heartbeats arranged by beds of roses in full bloom
Don't expect much of her
There's rain beneath her wings after midnight
She bookmarks her good days when the bad ones speak in dust

They say everyone makes mistakes,
but do they know about what it is to turn in a pair of rosy cheeks for a
collapse of soul?
Have they made the mistake of watching sugar harden to rage?
And air is one of the building blocks of life,
But I knocked that nonsense down with muddy boots and bartered with
smokes
They say everyone makes mistakes,
but have they ever made the mistake of painting their own beating heart in a
still-life, almost swearing they could see the paint pulsing?
And Death makes no attempt at formal introductions,
and you go zero to crazy in under two seconds?
They say everyone makes mistakes,
but have they ever lightly pawed a vase full of the blooms
of their soul off the edge of their bedside table,
so they'd no longer have to watch petals fall because they forgot to keep
them well hydrated?
They say everyone makes mistakes,
but have they ever been poor at taking care of their skin?
Forgetting to wash their face and holding up a 20 times magnified mirror
only to see pores clogged with distilled rain?
I could invest on a charcoal mask,
but that won't exfoliate grief well enough
They say everyone makes mistakes,
but have they ever looked to cigarette smoke to soak their thoughts in, then
hang them to dry on the lines of their face?
They say everyone makes mistakes,
but have they ever felt a sort of wild ecstasy at the sight of bones,
hips that seem to find the corner of every surface,
and you become expert at hiding bruises resulting from starvation-induced
clumsiness?
They say everyone makes mistakes....I have a library FULL of tombstone
mistakes
I hope you'll bring me flowers

Friday nights staggered over tombstones,
humming lullabies to the dead, bottle in hand
Mind-space is not playing nicely tonight
Stone angels kissed by moonlighted blues
Sapphire-choking
Lapis-soaking
Azure-poking cadavers because Heaven and Hell are busy at this time
Just in time for Sunday prayer, these poor blue-collared souls
And with half-hearted hands pressed together,
I utter something short of prayer but more than wishes,
that the night will be kinder to all my scattered skin patterns
beneath vague attitudes of blackened Fridays

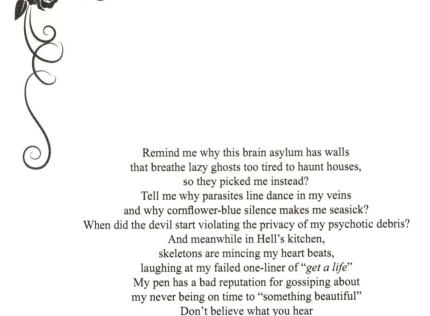

Remind me why this brain asylum has walls
that breathe lazy ghosts too tired to haunt houses,
so they picked me instead?
Tell me why parasites line dance in my veins
and why cornflower-blue silence makes me seasick?
When did the devil start violating the privacy of my psychotic debris?
And meanwhile in Hell's kitchen,
skeletons are mincing my heart beats,
laughing at my failed one-liner of *"get a life"*
My pen has a bad reputation for gossiping about
my never being on time to "something beautiful"
Don't believe what you hear

And so the prose goes
Using toothpicks to pick stars from my teeth
when chewing on universal pain
Unpolished, unrefined granules of raw, biting, jaw-clenched anonymous storm
rivulets of precipitated acid-jargon,
freshly squeezed from cumulus-rage consciousness
And laughter is sacred, but I dream of knives,
cocaine that may leave me at kite altitudes or Death's fathoms
Blessed are the souls who remain morning glory-open to whatever end
I lust after barstools, smoke ring visitors to Siamese lungs,
and morning after pillows,
Hangover-saturated with soot-filmy fingers bent
in an A-okay hand gesture
Rotting are the fruits of my written labors
Fermented language regulations thrown to the wind
Trigger-happy
Kiss
Bang
Dead

Black flannel top matches the shades beneath my chest today
Ankle boots, not certain if that's onyx or ebony, but either are tones of me at 4:21 pm
Distracted by the plagues of October, but my expression is cheerless in an idling car when the birds outside my window won't greet me in song
Last time I checked, I was still haunted
Veins, licorice-spun
Slate-blooded
Thoughts are sable-hued, soot-flavored
Heart thump thump thumps frigid tar, and I respect the black
I respect the black

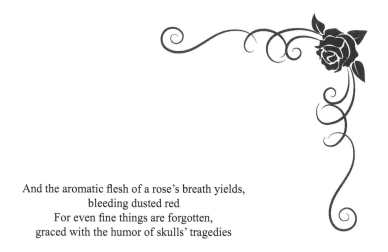

And the aromatic flesh of a rose's breath yields,
bleeding dusted red
For even fine things are forgotten,
graced with the humor of skulls' tragedies

ON REGROWTH...

Healing is making the bed every day to discourage chaos
Red brushstrokes over black granite blood
Healing is erasing the corpses of their names from the back of my chest wall,
leaving smears of crimson in their wake,
hand me down nightmares long after my soul has evolved
Healing is entertaining the idea of angel's wings
but only on Halloween because heaven would name me an impostor
I'll get those back some day
Healing is sympathizing with the pen of my younger self
Erratic, spirit-confetti strewn on torn-out pages
Healing is savoring my morning tea,
when the only bliss I can handle comes in yellow packet form
Healing is enduring his male gaze, void of voyeurism,
brim-filled with worship when my bloodstreams go cold in my nude state
Healing is my inner chant with that lesser than light self saying,
"If we should die today, let us be beautiful."

FIN.

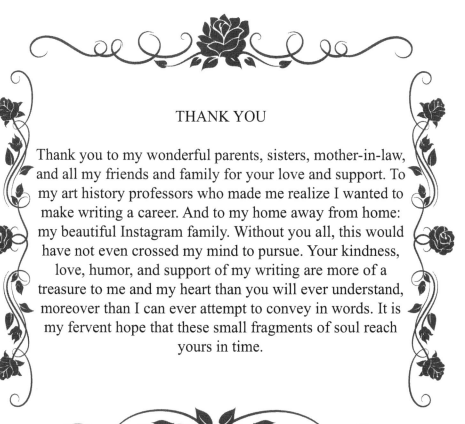

THANK YOU

Thank you to my wonderful parents, sisters, mother-in-law, and all my friends and family for your love and support. To my art history professors who made me realize I wanted to make writing a career. And to my home away from home: my beautiful Instagram family. Without you all, this would have not even crossed my mind to pursue. Your kindness, love, humor, and support of my writing are more of a treasure to me and my heart than you will ever understand, moreover than I can ever attempt to convey in words. It is my fervent hope that these small fragments of soul reach yours in time.

copyright © 2019 L.R.Sterling
"Apothecary Bloom"
All rights reserved. No part of this publication may be reproduced, distributed, conveyed or used in any manner without the express written permission of the author.

All literary works inside this publication were written and produced by L.R. Sterling.

Editor: L.R. Sterling & Derek Thorne
Photography: Pause Imaging
Digital Art Director: Covy Phelps

ISBN: 9781707520626

You can find more of the work of L.R. Sterling on Instagram:
@TheTasteOfMyPen

Or use the QR code on the back of this book.

Made in the USA
Columbia, SC
25 February 2020